STORY MAKER

Write Your Own Story Book

By Tyler David

Title: *Write Your Own Story Book*
Author: Tyler David

Published by: Books Boost Business.com
Registered in England & Wales No. 15505569
Books Boost Business Ltd
71-75, Shelton Street,
Covent Garden, London, WC2H 9JQ

ISBN: 978-1-917288-00-2

This book is a work of fiction. Names, characters, places, and incidents are either the product of the author's imagination or used fictitiously. Any resemblance to actual events, locales, or persons, living or dead, is purely coincidental.

BOOKS BOOST BUSINESS
"You should write a book about that"

Introduction

Hi! I'm Tyler David, and I started writing books when I was just 4 years old. Now I've written over 40 books, and guess what? You can do it too!

In this book, YOU are the author! You get to create your own amazing adventure by answering fun questions and drawing your best ideas. Is your main character a person, an animal, or even a robot made of marshmallows? It's all up to you!

By the end, you'll have written your very own book! How cool is that? So, grab a pencil and let's get started! I can't wait to see what amazing stories you create. Let your imagination run wild!

Author/Pen Name:__________________________________

Main Character Creation

It's time to make your main character! This is where the fun really starts.

Who is your main character? Are they a person, a magical animal, or something completely new? Maybe they're big and furry, or tiny and shiny—who knows?

____

____

What's their name? ______________________________

What do they look like? ____________________________

Are they funny, brave, or a bit of both? ________________

Let your imagination run free and draw your main character right here. I can't wait to see who you come up with!

Where the Story Begins

Now that you have your main character, let's figure out where their adventure starts! It can be anywhere you want.

Does your character live in a treehouse in the clouds?

Or maybe in a magical castle by the sea?

Could they be on a spaceship zooming through space, or in a tiny house in the forest?

Wherever it is, you get to decide! Draw the place where your story begins. I'm so excited to see where your adventure takes us!

The Problem or Challenge

Every good story has a problem or a mystery—now it's time for your main character to face theirs!

What's the big problem in your story?

Has something gone missing?

Does a friend need help?

Or did your character find a secret that needs solving?

Who or what is making things tricky for your main character?

Is it a sneaky villain or something else?

Write down or draw what makes things difficult for your character.

____

____

Adventure Time

Every adventure needs a little help! What three things does your main character take with them on their journey?

Are they magical tools?

Powerful gadgets?

Or maybe some super cool friends to help out?

Think about what your character might need—maybe a magic wand or a talking animal friend! Draw the special things or friends that will help your character on their adventure.

The Unexpected Twist

Uh-oh! Something surprising happens! Every great story has a twist. What will happen in yours?

Does your character find a secret door?

Maybe a new friend turns out to be an enemy?

Or they discover hidden treasure!

How does your character feel? Are they surprised, excited, or scared? And what do they do next? Draw or write about the big surprise!

____

____

The Big Moment

This is the most exciting part of your story! Your main character is about to face their biggest challenge.

What will they do?

Will they come up with a clever plan?

Or use something they found earlier on the adventure?

How does your character handle the big moment? Draw or write about the most exciting part of the story. Let's make this part really thrilling!

____

____

Wow, you’ve created an amazing story! Now it’s time to design your very own book cover.

Imagine you’re an artist designing the cover to show everyone just how exciting your story is. Think about what makes your adventure special—maybe it’s your main character, the place they went, or the surprise twist!

What colours will you use to make it stand out?

Will you draw your main character, or maybe a big moment from your story?

What title would you give your story?

Grab your pencils, crayons, or paints and draw your front cover right here. When you're done, hold up your book and say, "I am an author!"

You Did It! Congratulations!

Wow, you've just finished your very own story!

You've been an amazing author, creating characters, places, and adventures all from your imagination. But guess what? The adventure doesn't stop here!

Want to turn your story into a real book you can hold in your hands?

Scan the QR code to join Tyler's awesome online workshops where you can learn how to make your story into a real printed book! It's fun, exciting, and perfect for all young authors like you!

For Parents:

Your child has completed a wonderful journey of creativity, and now there's an exciting opportunity for them to take it even further.

By scanning the QR code, your child can join Tyler David's online workshops to turn their story into a printed book—an experience that boosts creativity and confidence.

As a thank you for purchasing this book, use the discount code included with the workshops. These books make great keepsakes and thoughtful gifts for family and friends. Watch your child's confidence grow as they create something truly special!

MY STORY,
MY ADVENTURE!

Books Featured....

i News
BARNES & NOBLE
Waterstones
WHSmith
Harvard Book Store SINCE 1932
ULTRA EDUCATION
sky
Agendabookshop
Walmart
FOREVER FAMILY FOREVER FREE
TruLittle Hero Awards

Business success recognition awards 2022
D&R MUSIC BOOK STORE
goodreads
FOYLES
ebay
DYMOCKS books & gifts
Browns Books
AbeBooks.com
wheelers for schools
hive.co.uk
ab
BIBLIO
PRINCE BOOKS
Sandman Book Company
BOOKS WAGON
Indigo
Kings books
the intellectual bookshop
AN ONLINE BOOKSTORE FOR CHILDREN
OFF THE BEATEN PATH
GOOD BOOKS, GOOD COFFEE, GOOD FRIENDS.
QUEEN ANNE BOOK COMPANY

More Amazing Books!

KIDS GET LEARNING

Printed in Great Britain
by Amazon

51312976R00015